GOODBYE SALAD DAYS

GOODBYE SALAD DAYS

KEVIN FACES ADULTHOOD

BY TRAER SCOTT

CHRONICLE BOOKS
SAN FRANCISCO

For Agatha and Jesse.
Serendipity is real-life magic.

Kevin thinks maybe a trip to the
playa will spark some spiritual awakening
through radical self-expression.

Or he'll just be dehydrated and
surrounded by weirdos.

These days Kevin's abs look more like a pony
keg than a six-pack, so he decides to renew his gym
membership and hit the weights.

He is sure that he can't stay out drinking
all night and still make it to work in the morning,
and he is definitely not going to do it again.

Kevin tells himself this every time.

After having a few beers, Kevin decides to recapture
the carefree feeling of youth with a good swing!

According to his therapist, artistic hobbies are a healthy
way of channeling emotions.

Kevin signed up for a pottery class, and it's going pretty well.

Kevin's succulent died.

No one warned him about overwatering.

Is this a metaphor?

Kevin spots his first gray hair.

Is baldness imminent?

His mom keeps asking whether she's
going to get any grandchildren.

Kevin's dating apps aren't so sure.

Kevin thought perhaps ice fishing would help him get in touch with his masculinity through stoic solitude and oneness with nature.

Kevin was wrong.

Kevin is starting to wonder if this is it.

Is he going to sit here at this desk for
the rest of his life?

Kevin has realized saving for
retirement is something he's supposed
to be doing like, right now

Owning a home is much less satisfying
than he thought it would be.

Stoic solitude was a bust, so Kevin's
going to try to get in touch with his need
for speed instead.

All this new technology is
starting to feel threatening, so Kevin
heads out for an analog activity.

Very vintage.

Kevin suddenly finds himself being
expected to mentor the younger hires.

Wasn't he just the younger hire?

What the hell is fabric softener,
and why are there 40 different kinds
of laundry detergent to pick from?

He's starting to wonder if getting
rid of everything that doesn't spark joy
would mean an empty house. . . .

Kevin isn't sure if he lacks
sensitivity and creativity,
but he's pretty sure he can
splatter paint himself.

Should he have a kid so he
can go trick-or-treating again
without it being weird?

What does having an exaggerated sense
of attachment to childhood relics mean?

Kevin calls his therapist the next day.

He spent all weekend binge-watching his favorite show and now it's over.

He feels empty.

Kevin considers getting a pet,
but thinks back to the succulent disaster.

Kevin embarks on a spiritual quest to
try and find the meaning of life.

Why *are* we here?

Also, now he's *sure* the exercise isn't working.

It was a steep hike.

Kevin let his mom set him up on a blind date.

It did not go well.

He can't believe he just paid $12
for avocado toast.

Kevin doesn't know what happened, but he's
pretty sure he used to be cool.

Maybe it's time to get the band back together.

Hamsters are massively underrated creatures. They are much more adventurous, companionable, and enthralling than people think. My daughter's kindergarten classroom was home to the beloved Professor Pickles and we, like several other families, allowed ourselves to be cajoled into getting a hamster. We are animal people. We have dogs, fish, and other periodic menagerie guests so I am always up for another furry friend, but there were two things I didn't realize about hamsters: 1) They are a fair amount of work. 2) They are fascinating and deserve much more respect than they get.

Hamsters are often referred to as "starter pets" and this designation makes me cringe because they are wonderfully sentient animals that need mental stimulation, daily exercise, and attention. Unfortunately, their lives are short. Even the most well-cared-for hamster is unlikely to see its third year. This is one of many reasons that they are sold for less than the price of two grande lattes at chain pet supply stores.

I believe in always pursuing adoption first, so we tried to find an adoptable hammy in our area, but there were none at the time. Guinea pigs and rabbits are much more common in shelters and rescues, primarily because their lifespans are considerably longer. Buying your hamster directly from a reputable breeder is a good option, but upon Googling it, you will most likely find, as we did, that the nearest hamster breeder is 1000 miles away, and of course no reputable breeder would subject their animals to shipping.

Ultimately, when neither of these preferable options are viable, people turn to chain pet supply stores to purchase rodent pets. Without naming names, I will say that not all of these companies are created equal and it's important to be a responsible consumer: Research where the animals they sell come from and find out about their return/vet care policy. A responsible, caring company should be transparent about their sources and also offer professional vet care and treatment of any animal they sell that should become sick, at no cost to you.

Our first hamster, Nibbles, was very young when we got him and for the first week he just hid. This is normal, but disappointing for a young child who expects a pet that will instantly like them. We gave him his space, took it slow, and eventually he became the friendliest, most affectionate little rodent. Every night at sundown, he would emerge from sleep and stand on his hind feet, and then come up to the front of the cage, signaling that he was ready to come out. We would hold him, pet him, and then put him, in his ball so he could roll around the house for an hour or so. Hamsters absolutely love exploring.

My daughter and Nibbles soon formed a close relationship. She would build little "worlds" for him to explore and he would reward us with unending feats of hamster ability. All hamsters have cheek pouches that stretch all the way back to their shoulders. They use these to carry food and/or bedding from one place to another. The insides of the cheek pouches are completely dry so if they stuff them full of say, toilet paper to make a nest out of, when they unload it, it will be fresh and dry. Watching a hamster fill its cheek pouches with carrots or other veggies is one of the most endearing and comical things you can witness. They can fit an enormous amount in these spacious pouches. Our Syrian hamsters can put one good-sized baby carrot in each pouch, effectively widening their girth by about two inches.

It's important to remember that hamsters are prey animals, which means that they are uncomfortable and nervous in wide-open spaces. A hamster is much happier nestled under a little hut, inside a toilet paper roll, or buried under bedding. One of the places that my daughter thought to put

Nibbles was in her dollhouse. Perhaps because it was enclosed and somewhat cavernous, he really liked it. He began scampering around from room to room, trying out the beds, smelling everything, and even climbing the stairs. When I first saw him in there I took a quick snap with my phone because it was bizarre and irresistible. I posted it on Instagram and got an over-whelming response. Apparently, everyone else loved it as much as I did.

It took a few weeks for me to connect the dots, but eventually it became clear that we had happened upon something too wonderful not to share with the world. A little brainstorming and tweaking and *Goodbye Salad Days* was born.

Photography has become infinitely less corporal since I began, twenty-five years ago. My hands used to smell of developer and fixer, and images didn't exist until they showed up as negatives on film. Now, many or most images live a purely digital life. A half-life, in my opinion. One of the beautiful things about making books is that I, and the reader, can have something tangible to hold in our hands. But I still miss the physicality of the darkroom, and of my early career when I made props, sewed costumes, and built sets.

I am a career photographer, but I also have a wide and varied art background that includes a little bit of knowledge and experience in a vast number of mediums: sculpture, painting, drawing, pottery, felting, costume and set design to name a few. I have looked for ways to incorporate some of these disciplines into my photography, but all have seemed forced until this project. *Goodbye Salad Days* gave me a wonderful chance to unleash all of my creativity and skills in a whimsical, and harm-lessly puerile way. What could be more fun?

Some of these sets are inspired by real places that I have been. The Blind Date restaurant was modeled directly after a beautiful little French café in Old Town Montreal. Kevin's kitchen was loosely inspired by the fabulous London vegan restaurant Pharmacy. But for the most part, they all just came out of my mind, piece by piece. I would start with a color, or one piece of furniture, or one prop, and build from there. I made many of the props myself as it rather impossible to find 1:12 scale dying succulents, empty French wine bottles, bean bag chairs, shower curtains, and so on. I got to sculpt, sew, glue, and paint. All of the original artwork featured in the sets (like that of the art museum and mother's house) were done by me. There are also numerous references to two of my daughter's and my favorite things: The Beatles and *Harry Potter*.

I could not have made these sets without the help of my husband, who can build, fix, and engineer just about anything from nothing. I am very good at being creative but really lousy at things like measurements, carpentry, and abstract math. This book was very much a family effort. We built these sets as a family, and we shot them together as well. Shooting with creatures requires at least one assistant. My daughter and husband were hamster wranglers, dangling pieces of grapes on strings from chopsticks in order to get him to go one place or another.

People keep asking how we make the hamsters do these things. The answer is that we don't make the hamsters do anything. All we do is put them in the dioramas and then offer food rewards that direct them to this side or that. The rest is just their natural behavior, instinct, and personality. Many of these scenarios were in fact designed with the natural instincts of the hamster in mind. For example, hamsters love swings so it made sense to have a swing scene. Hamsters love to climb, so a mountain is perfect. Hamsters love to stand on their hind legs and pause, seemingly perplexed or lost in thought, so many scenes were designed with that look in mind. Not only would it be inhumane to force a hamster to do something against their nature, I think it would be fairly impossible—and would certainly yield horrible photos.

So, my disclaimer cum mantra for *Goodbye Salad Days* is as follows:

No hamsters were harmed in the making of this book.
All hamsters received nutritious compensation for their efforts.
All hamsters in this book are beloved family pets.
You should probably not try this at home.

Goodbye Salad Days is an odd little offering, particularly within the context of the rest of my books, but for me, it meant a joining of many things that I love. In several speaking engagements I have mentioned that this was the hardest project I have ever done, which is pretty laughable given my resume, but it's true. Building little worlds takes an attention to detail that is innate in me, but the planning is much easier than the execution. I am a photographer, not a miniaturist, so every single diorama meant a host of new skills that I had to master. I am also now a PhD in rodent psychology, hamster cuisine, and general small animal care. I hope that Kevin's story will continue, but whether it does or not, I will be forever grateful for the serendipity that brought hamsters into our life and inspired yet another creative chapter.

Acknowledgements

So many people believed in this weird little book, and I need to heartily thank them. First, Josse, without whose expert skills in carpentry and hamster wrangling this project would not have existed. Thank you to my amazing and indefatigable agent, Joan Brookbank, for always supporting my ideas, no matter how bizarre, and for being the best matchmaker between artist and editor. Which leads me to Becca Hunt, my editor at Chronicle, who championed this book from its first breath and was utterly in sync with my vision for it from concept to completion. I am so grateful to have been paired with you. To Leigh Saffold and Olivia Roberts for being so thorough, patient, and an absolute joy to work with. Many thanks to Maggie Edelman for her fantastic design. Finally, thank you to Alison Petersen, Tom Fernald, and Christine Carswell at Chronicle.

Special thanks to Sean Bennett Dessureau for his unrelenting commitment to the cause of hamster laundry detergent.

And of course, thank you to my daughter Agatha who had the genius idea of putting our hamster in her dollhouse so that he could explore a new world.

Library of Congress Cataloging-in-Publication Data available.

ISBN: 978-1-4521-8193-6

Manufactured in China.

10 9 8 7 6 5 4 3 2 1

Chronicle books and gifts are available at special quantity discounts to
corporations, professional associations, literacy programs, and other organizations.
For details and discount information, please contact our premiums department at
corporatesales@chroniclebooks.com or at 1-800-759-0190.

Chronicle Books LLC
680 Second Street
San Francisco, California 94107

www.chroniclebooks.com